Journey to My Self

What My Inner Shaman, My Grandma
and a host of Otherworld Beings
Taught Me About Courage, Creativity and
Reclaiming My Power

Karen Klein

BALBOA.
PRESS
A DIVISION OF HAY HOUSE

Balboa Press books may be ordered through booksellers or by contacting:

Balboa Press
A Division of Hay House
1663 Liberty Drive
Bloomington, IN 47403
www.balboapress.com
1 (877) 407-4847

Because of the dynamic nature of the Internet, any web addresses or links contained in this book may have changed since publication and may no longer be valid. The views expressed in this work are solely those of the author and do not necessarily reflect the views of the publisher, and the publisher hereby disclaims any responsibility for them.

The author of this book does not dispense medical advice or prescribe the use of any technique as a form of treatment for physical, emotional, or medical problems without the advice of a physician, either directly or indirectly. The intent of the author is only to offer information of a general nature to help you in your quest for emotional and spiritual well-being. In the event you use any of the information in this book for yourself, which is your constitutional right, the author and the publisher assume no responsibility for your actions.

Print information available on the last page.

ISBN: 978-1-5043-5152-2 (sc)
ISBN: 978-1-5043-5154-6 (hc)
ISBN: 978-1-5043-5153-9 (e)

Library of Congress Control Number: 2016902904

Balboa Press rev. date: 03/11/2016

A NOTE FROM THE AUTHOR

I spent years searching to find my spiritual path, although I didn't know that that was what I was looking for. I was aware of my spiritual void, but I didn't know how to fill that void. My family's religious tradition was a liberal protestant church, so I started there. I went on to explore traditional and nontraditional religions; I read books, went to classes about spiritual awakening, and became a Reiki master. Oftentimes I would conclude, *no, that's not working for me.* Yet I was compelled to continue my search and ended up in a very different place, an empowering spiritual realm and creative source that I had no idea even existed.

In this heretofore-unknown place, I found my Inner Shaman, who helped me crack open layers of my authentic Self. It was a strange experience that required trust in something I knew nothing about. But time and again, visit after visit, the Shaman led me to new knowledge, new acceptance, and a deeper understanding of my Self. From the first encounter to an understanding of the powerful connection I now have, I am grateful that I allowed myself to participate. I now know that when I get off course (because that's the human condition), there is a resource within me that I can rely on to bring me back to center.

When I was finalizing my manuscript for this book, in the middle of the night I had the realization that the chakra colors were present in this journey from the very beginning. The Sanskrit word *chakra* literally translates to wheel or disk. In yoga, meditation, and Ayurveda, this term refers to wheels of energy throughout the body. There are seven main chakras, starting from the base of the spine and going to the crown of the head.

The chakra colors were introduced to me separately but had very significant meanings for the events that were occurring in my life. (In case you are not familiar with the chakras and the chakra colors, I have included a brief explanation in the appendix. I will also tell you that I knew nothing of chakra colors prior to my Reiki experience.)

I am sharing my experience in the hope that you can find this powerful healing resource within you as well.

One of the most important things I want readers to know is that I created the photography in this book ten years before my Shamanic Journeys began. I realize now that the images were my first journey into exploring my hunger for Self. Later in *Journey to My Self*, I would recreate these images in words. Imagine my surprise and delight at being able to fuse the two together.

And so it is.

Karen Klein

ACKNOWLEDGEMENTS

Thank you to Kathy Shay and the Spiritual Memoir Workshop participants: your encouragement helped me to see this book as a possibility.

Also, much gratitude to my great-grandfather, my grandma, my parents, and to Julie, Zan, Donna, Betsy, John, Krissa, Lisa, Kathy, Annie, Suzanne, Lucy, Cheri, Mike, Phyllis, and everyone else who listened to me talk about my amazing adventure.

Thank you, Annie Wilder of Inkswiggler Editing & Publishing Consults, for the developmental editing of my manuscript.

My mother left Earth on December 14, 2003. After that phone call from her nursing home, I felt like an orphan—an old one, but an orphan nonetheless. I was aware of a dramatic shift on a deep level. I mourned and grieved, gathered my family, and memorialized her life with a slideshow I put together from that huge box of photographs she had moved so many times. As I was growing up, whenever the family gathered, a drawer filled with photographs of our relatives would be put on the dining room table for all of us to look at again. In that experience, we asked questions and retold our family's stories. Now those photos had another purpose. A beautifully haunting violin solo of "Amazing Grace" accompanied the slideshow. I felt that my mother would have liked the tribute—so complete in its simplicity.

Then I got back to working at my job, getting on with my life as I knew it.

I received my degree in studio arts in 1988, but as soon as I had that piece of paper, I went to work in the "real world." For lack of time and energy, I did none of my own art during my employment. In 2005, I decided to retire and focus all my energies on my artwork. I understood that time is precious and whatever of my time remained, I was going to spend it on my artwork, not the nine-to-five. When I disconnected from my work life and focused on my art, many personal concerns, interests, and questions arose. One of them was my spiritual void, bankruptcy, blank—something that had started after my mother's transition into spirit. Now it seemed to demand my attention.

A journalist published a weekly column called "The Seeker's Diary" in the local newspaper. He attended a different church every week and wrote about what he found there—the environment and the experience of worship. I started to follow his lead, attending church after church to find a place that would resonate with me.

I was seriously working on my art, learning about digital cameras and Photoshop. The more I worked and learned, the more productive and experimental I became. The art I was making was indeed personal and deeply satisfying.

Over time, I created a body of work that I titled *In Focus, Out of Memory*. It eventually consisted of seventeen black-and-white images documenting my personal journey. With such titles as "She Knew Why, but Not When," "She Thought He'd Know," "She Had That Dream Again," this work became very important to me. The more I created, the more I could own my life experience. I submitted this work for exhibit at every opportunity. In 2010, it was selected for a two-person show at Monterey Peninsula College. That meant not only that my work would be matted and framed and shipped, but that I would have an artist's talk-and-meet with the photography students. *Yikes!* I was always afraid that my work wasn't good enough, so this was a significant validation I readily accepted.

Having had many good experiences with classes I had attended and books I had read, I continued my spiritual quest too. And I always sought more—more answers, more questions, and more experiences.

During this period, after a fitful night of sleep, I awakened with an image that I needed to draw. I fumbled for my notebook and pen and sketched a little girl walking with her hand in an adult's hand. I had no idea what it meant, but I understood I needed to record it. That was in the fall of 2011. Now I realize it was foretelling of things to come.

I was browsing away at a used bookstore—looking for the answers to what I felt was my spiritual bankruptcy. In the metaphysical section, I came across a book titled *Personal Mythology.*[1] *I picked it up, and on the lavender cover, I read the subtitle: Use Ritual, Dreams, and Imagination to Discover Your Inner Story.* Sounded good to me, and for $5.48, I

---

[1]   David Feinstein, PhD and Stanley Krippner, PhD, *Personal Mythology: Using Ritual, Dreams, and Imagination to Discover Your Inner Story* (Los Angeles: Jeremy P. Tarcher, Inc., 1988).

was on to a new experience. I took the book home and embraced the possibilities it offered (even though I wasn't sure what they were). I truly believed that anything would be better than where I was in my endless and fruitless search to "own" my spirituality.

I curled up in my favorite stuffed chair and began paging through the prologue, "Expanding Your Mythology Beyond Limiting Cultural Images." There were suggestions to use a personal journal, instructions on guided imagery and working with dreams, and tips on overcoming resistance. All of this was new and acceptable to me. I eagerly turned to chapter 1, "Into Your Mythic Depths." It began with a quote from Joseph Campbell: "It has always been the prime function of mythology and rite to supply the symbols that move the human spirit forward." To my hungry mind, it just kept getting better and better!

The third paragraph header was "A Journey Back to Your Ancestors." The guided meditation, "Personal Ritual: Meeting Your Inner Shaman," said the Inner Shaman might be in the guise of a wise old man, the Earth Mother, a known master, a Celtic priestess, Jesus, Confucius, or whoever emerges into awareness. As the directions in the book stated, "The Inner Shaman is not revealed to the unprepared or casual seeker."

And so it was, the fall of 2011 marked the beginning of my Inner Shaman journeys. I went about setting up my meditation space with candles. Per instructions, I closed my eyes and followed the directions to locate myself in a timeless and dreamlike reality, then to follow a path into the dark places of my being.

Fall 2011: First Visit

I am slowly walking on a dirt path. It is very worn; the dirt is dark and hard, but smooth and cool. I appear younger than I am now (maybe in my twenties), and my hair color is darker. I am barefoot and wearing a light colored, mid-calf '60s-era, flower-patterned cotton dress.

One cautious step after another leads me to a clearing surrounded by lush green plants with trees on the left side. It is very beautiful in the natural disorder of nature with bamboo, birch, eucalyptus, many varieties of fern, blooming magnolias, hibiscus, orchids, and wild roses everywhere. All the shades of green foliage, the peeling white bark of the birch, the multitude of the blooms burst forth to present an orgy of color. There is a sweet, fresh scent that I breathe in deeply and slowly. On the right side, there lies a dark, small body of water, like a swamp. On the banks are lots of tangled roots and large-leafed dark growth, all uninviting and ominous.

At the end of the path, there are two willow trees, one on each side, with long, hanging branches forming an archway to the shaman's door. The door appears to be in the middle of a large mound of dirt that is completely covered with vines of dark-green ivy. As I approach the door, I see it is made of vertical planks of old, faded, gray wood. I am reminded of the weathered wood from the barn on the farm where I grew up.

I lift my right hand and gently knock. My inner guide tells me my password phrase: "I am because I create," and after I say it, the shaman opens the door. I enter a large, round space filled with warm, golden light. I look up and see that it is open—there is no roof, no ceiling, no sky—just open to the infinite. The energy is palpable, and I experience joy and awe, a nice replacement for my usual anxieties.

When I was little, my paternal grandparents lived with us, so I had an awareness of an extended family whose names, stories, and photographs were familiar to me. In seeking an ancestor, I knew the ancestor I would most relate to was my great-grandfather Karl Emil Otto. In the drawer of family photos, I had seen pictures of him with his family and his students. His roll-top desk is now in my living room. At the age of twenty-eight, he was sent from Mansfeld, Germany, to Wisconsin to minister to the immigrant farmers. He arrived in Milwaukee on April 29, 1865, and from that humble beginning, he went on to become the president of Eden Seminary in Marthasville, Missouri, and a professor of theology at Eden. At some point—and this is where he became my hero—the synod asked him to leave because in his classroom he taught and encouraged a "symbolical method of Scripture interpretation."[2] Indeed this is a very shortened, distilled version of his teaching and the

[2]   Lowell H. Zuck, *Evangelical Pietism and Biblical Criticism: The Story of Karl Emil Otto*, http://www.ucc.org/about-us_hidden-histories-2_evangelical-pietism-and.

event at Eden; my point is that I revered his commitment to his truth. Eventually his teachings were reconsidered. He went on to serve many years as a minister and as a professor of ancient languages and history at Elmhurst College.

When I went to scatter my mom's ashes in Missouri, I stopped at Eden Seminary and met with the archivist. As soon as I entered the room, I saw my great-grandfather's picture on the wall of the archives in the basement of the library. I immediately recognized him. I knew he had a full beard and thick hair. I remembered that my dad sometimes referred to his grandpa as "Rot Otto," as his hair had a reddish cast. Today, in the Eden Seminary Chapel in St. Louis, Missouri, there is a stained-glass window dedicated to his memory. Something about my truth-seeking, rebellious great-grandfather was very important to me, so when the book's instructions were to introduce myself to my Inner Shaman via the meditation, I was very confident and excited to proceed.

Fall 2011: First Visit, Continued

Now I meet him as my Shaman, and he still has a thick beard and lots of coarse hair, but it is all white. He has pale blue eyes, just like mine are and my dad's were. I know he expects me, and he welcomes me by placing his hands on my shoulders. He looks directly into my eyes and smiles. Then he takes my hand, and I walk with him to the left. There are no words exchanged.

The golden light makes the inner space feel very welcoming and comfortable. The floor feels like hard earth. I am aware of the space feeling magical, like in a dream where walls are transparent. There is no sound or smell, but the air is charged with energy. I look around and see there is no roof, no ceiling, yet also not a blue sky but something beyond that—just space emanating golden light. The inner space feels very large, but without contents. I cannot see the other side, but in the middle of the space, I do see a very large mound of down feathers.

We proceed on our walk; first he leads me to the Creative Bush. It is tall and round, heavy with dark green foliage and blueberry-size red berries. He picks some berries and feeds them to me; they are sweet and juicy. He then gives me a spoonful of green liquid. I notice that it has no flavor.

He takes my hand, and we walk around to a rocker where my beloved Grandma Klein (his daughter, Clara) is sitting! I am so happy to see her—my saving grace when I was a little girl. She and Grandpa Klein lived with us, and she always had time to play with me, either making shadow puppets on the wall in their room or playing house with my dolls. Her lap was a place of refuge and welcome. I hug her and sit down next to her; her love envelopes me just like when I was a little girl sitting on her lap while she rocked me, stroked my brow, and assured me that all was well. I thank the Shaman and leave.

I found my first experience with my Inner Shaman exhilarating—visually powerful and very safe. I knew I would repeat this, and now it is part of my early morning ritual.

Fall 2011: Second Visit

A few days after my first visit to the Inner Shaman, I follow the same routine. I walk the path to the door, knock, say the password; the door opens, and there he is. This visit, I observe myself as a young girl, little Karen, about five or six, who was sexually abused by a male cousin five years older than she. I take her to my Grandma Klein, who is slowly rocking back and forth, seemingly waiting for me to arrive with the child. She reaches out for the pale child (me), puts her on her lap, and rocks her, stroking her hair and reassuring her that she's okay now. Later, I see them making shadow puppets on the wall by the light of the kerosene lamp.

I did not start this meditation with the intent to bring forth this part of me. It happened; I believe the Inner Shaman knew I needed to heal this part of me, so this "little Karen" appeared. Over the years, I had discussed this issue in therapy—many different kinds of talk therapy. And I never escaped the cloud of knowing I was different. I had lost innocence; I had been robbed of discovering my sexuality as a positive, joyful part of me.

Fall 2011: Third Visit

The next time I go to the Inner Shaman, after the welcome and walk to the Creative Bush, he leads me to a dark, damp hiding place on the left side of the pile of down. I have not been this far around the space before, but now I see there are two more little Karens cowering under a large canopy of dark leaves. I sense their fear and their shame. This dark, dank place seems connected to the dark water stream that is outside by the path to the entrance.

The five-year-old had received a wounding message in kindergarten—a comment from a piano teacher during a lesson: "You are the most …" and my five-year-old self immediately knew, by the tone she used, that whatever that word was, it wasn't good; I was hurt and ashamed. The other Karen was hurt by a thoughtless remark at age eight. While I was singing Christmas carols with a cousin who was playing the piano for our duet, my dad had walked into the room. "You can't sing," he said, laughing at my efforts before leaving.

I didn't want to take piano lessons, but I did—for twelve years. I wanted to take dancing lessons, but my mother thought that was too sexual, so I couldn't do that. And I have never enjoyed singing. The self-consciousness I absorbed from both of these events impacted me greatly; I am slowly healing. I felt that my discoveries with the Inner Shaman let me own and know myself, even the parts that were frustrating and self-defeating.

In early December 2011, after a twenty-plus year marriage, I moved out of our marital residence into my own apartment. This was a second marriage for both of us, and many things came into play.

She Took Nothing and Everything

My granddaughter had lived with us from age ten to eighteen, then she started college and moved to campus. My husband and I had her to absorb our attention, and after she moved out, we faced the dilemma of sitting across the table with nothing to say. I was more and more absorbed in my art and felt a separate space would be best for both of us. I found my little apartment (a room of one's own) to be perfect for my art, my evolving journey, and me.

Early December 2011

The next time I visit the Inner Shaman, he greets me, then blesses me with light, knowledge, peace, and insight—kind of a '60s thing. As I leave, I see my six grandchildren standing alongside the path, waiting for me —all smiles, and all of the same age, maybe nine? I realize that it is always daylight and warm here; I never thought about that before, but I am so grateful since the dark winters make me so depressed.

December 29, 2011

I take the infant girl my mother birthed at 6:05 a.m. on December 29, 1942—me—to the Inner Shaman. I follow the path to the plank door, knock, and say "I am because I create," then he opens the door. He smiles, and I show him the infant Karen. He takes her/me and holds her in his arms, shifts her to his shoulder, and rubs her back. He returns her to me, and I take her in my arms, where she is quickly absorbed into my body. My first thought is, "Now I am complete, and I can nourish her, and we will make really fine art together!"

I remember hearing my mother say she thought I was hungry all the time, from the moment I was born. At that time, babies were fed on schedule, not demand. I probably was hungry and did my best to make that known, but she wouldn't disobey her doctor's orders about the feeding schedule.

January 1, 2012

On this visit, I bring my infant Karen with me again. My Inner Shaman takes my hand and we walk to the left, first to eat berries from the Creative Bush then on to whatever adventure/information/education he has for me. This time, we go to Grandma, who is slowly rocking and telling stories to the growing group of little Karens. They vary in age a little, but they all wear the same little royal-blue cotton dress with a sailor collar, patent leather shoes, and white anklets. I give Grandma the infant Karen. She takes the infant and begins to breast-feed her.

I am always enchanted by the magic here; there is no unbuttoning a dress or fumbling with a bra, the old woman simply offers her milk-filled breast—it just is. I leave the infant with Grandma, knowing that she will nurture and nourish me/her to health.

The Shaman and I continue walking till we reach a doorway that opens to a large, open white space where there is a tree, maybe a banyan tree. The trunk resembles intertwined torsos, the branches are like arms reaching up, while the roots are firmly planted and growing down, into the earth. My Shaman and I sit under the tree, and he gives me a cup of green liquid. I have had a spoonful previously, but now I drink a cupful, and it still has no taste. I have no idea what it is for, but I sit and gratefully drink it while gazing around my beautiful space, my Shaman's beautiful space.

I loved my new apartment; the location was within walking distance to the YWCA, a wonderful coffee shop, my favorite hair place, a co-op, and at least three really good restaurants. The only downside was that it was winter in Minnesota and I no longer had a garage. Also, the radiator heat in the old building was very drying, so I had three humidifiers and periodic nosebleeds. My kitchen was very small, but that didn't matter—I felt so removed from the need to cook.

And I revisited a photo project dealing with the effects of divorce on children; it took a lot of my time and energy, and that was a good thing. I had started the project in response to my own divorce in 1980. My first husband and I had three children, and after our divorce in 1980, I moved with them to Minneapolis from Florida. Our children were ten, fourteen, and seventeen at the time. Things did not go as I had imagined, and the divorce became a very painful experience for all of us.

In 1988, I was completing my MFA degree and decided to make the divorce and its consequences a part of my MFA thesis exhibit. I photographed young adults whose parents were divorced, and I interviewed them about that experience and how it affected them then and now. The photographs, along with their statements, became part of my exhibit.

Now, in 2012, I continued with this project, *Broken Circle—Children of Divorce and Separation.* Again I photographed young adults whose parents were divorced and interviewed them about that experience and how it affected them.

Late January 2012

During a later meditation, there appears a new vision— an energy of intense, bright white light. It appears beyond the large open white space where there wasn't anything previously. I am uncertain to the point of tears; what does this mean? I think it is female; the form is like two triangles meeting in the middle. My Shaman is there, but "she" dominates the space, and she keeps getting larger. And the light is blinding! At first I think I am transitioning, but to what? Success with my art? Death? The Shaman rests his hands on my shoulders to reassure me. All the light and beauty scare me, but I still want it. He must believe that I am ready to know this in spite of my fear. The white form slowly diminishes in size and brightness, and it magically relocates to a body of water that appears opposite the entrance. She floats there, and I know that her name is Clarity. The top half of her becomes a pale-blue color that pulsates in bands that appear to scroll up. Since her first appearance, she is always present, riding on that body of water. Sometimes she gets bigger and brighter, probably when I have clarity issues.

She Trusted Her Intuition

I also incorporated more self-care into my routine—yoga, Pilates, acupuncture, massage—all of which helped me feel connected to my Self. My search for a place to expand my spiritual self was ongoing, but I did find a church that I was comfortable with. It was started by three people who'd met at divinity school, was not affiliated with any religion, and "borrowed" space in other churches for Sunday evening services. It focused a lot on creativity, and the music at the services was a live band that played Americana gospel. The band consisted of professional musicians, and to me, was really inspiring. I knew that I went for the music, but the sermons were usually thought-provoking. I liked the whole experience there and it seemed a respite from my desperate search.

Late February 2012

The Shaman takes me first to the Creative Bush for the berries, and then we walk around to visit Grandma and the little Karens. All is well with them, so the Shaman and I continue on past the large white space with the banyan tree, past Clarity in all her radiant glory riding on the surface of the water, to an opening that leads directly to the beach. There is no door, just a large opening. I look out and see an expanse of white sand and a very calm body of turquoise water. We do not go out to the beach but continue walking and, suddenly, there is no more wall, only outside space. No door or entry, just open space, and in that space is a very tall sculpture. It is solid-looking, but I don't know the material. However, the colors are brilliant. It reminds me of Niki de Saint Phalle's work because of the size and colors. The Colorful Sculpture resembles two intertwined human forms, and it is pulsating with vibrant energy.

I was feeling more focused and more confident with my *Broken Circle* project, working with more clarity and confidence. A professional book designer offered to help with the logo and layout, pro bono, because he believed so strongly in the project. Gratitude had become part of my vocabulary too.

April 2012

In this visit, the large, solid Colorful Sculpture that had been such powerful presence melts before my eyes! The colors merge together and slide off the structure to the ground revealing a long, black, thin—what? A Star Wars light saber, perhaps? No; it's black and dark. I don't know what to make of any of it as I watch the black thing transform into an upright leafy vine. I watch the leafy vine grow into a tree, then suddenly it is at the right side of the Creative Bush, and it, too, has red berries. Then the red berries bloom into gold coins ... I understand that it is a Money Tree, next to the Creative Bush!

In my real world, I found out that I hadn't made the cut for a McKnight photo grant that would have helped me fund my *Broken Circle* project. I knew intellectually that rejection was always a possibility in the grant world, but emotionally it was crushing. I spent a lot of time wanting to throw out all my work and crying for myself, deeply crying, until

I decided I would just go to bed. Surprisingly, I slept well, and in the morning decided to see my Shaman.

May 2012

The first thing I notice is that the Shaman is sitting when I enter. I see Clarity riding on the water, but she's less dominant than usual. The Colorful Sculpture that had melted is back to its original form; the many intense colors are pulsing with energy again. The Shaman motions for me to sit on a chair in the middle of the space where the down pile had been. The walls are all a warm gold; perfect sunlight. I sit, basking in the warm, beautiful light, and suddenly another little Karen comes out of me—she steps out of my chest and goes to him. He puts her on his lap, and she cuddles into his shoulder. He is talking to her, and she is quiet and comfortable. Suddenly she starts pulling things— words, colors, I don't know what-all, but she pulls them out of her and throws them toward me, to the center of the space where I am sitting—and a fire starts! The word/color things burn up, as do I. I just melt, burn

away. The fire subsides, and she gets off the Shaman's

lap. As she walks toward the door, she grows from

the little girl into the adult me—a sixty-nine-year-old,

white-haired me instead of the younger version. I thank

the Shaman and leave.

I applied for, and did not receive, two other grants. This was very

difficult to accept, but again, I understood it was the nature of the beast.

I attended the review of my submission and saw the panel split about

the work I'd submitted. Hard to hear, but I knew the project had value

far beyond some of this panel's grasp.

Eary June 2012

On my next visit, everything in the interior seems dim,

not bright as usual. The Shaman motions for me to sit

on the down in the middle of the space, and when I

do, another little Karen emerges from me, and I watch

her proceed to sit on the "nest" of down. The down

doesn't float around and isn't messy like real down

feathers would be; it is just a large, deep, comfortable pile of down. After the child sits, she turns to gold and looks like a little Buddha girl. I understand that this transformation is to teach me patience. The little Buddha Karen stays there, and she morphs into me; she is in me and also on the down nest, learning and practicing patience. I glance to the right and see that the large Colorful Sculpture is spinning around in circles. It still looks like two human forms intertwined, but it is not writhing as before but rapidly spinning.

Late June 2012

It is in late June when I visit again, and the beautiful gold space enters me. It is in me as I am in it. It is my home, and my guides, the Shaman, Grandma Klein, Clarity, the Creative Bush, the Money Tree, the Colorful Sculpture, and all the little Karens are there for me. I still do not know what the green liquid is, but when the Shaman offers it to me, I drink it and again eat the red berries. I glance around and see that Clarity is very bright, with the pulsing, pale-blue light rising up into the universe—all good energy. I walk with the Shaman, and he leads me to the down feathers where the little Buddha Karen sits. He has me lie down there, and I am covered in gold coins. Then I rise up and continue walking around the space. Toward the back, on the side opposite the Creative Bush and leafy-stick-turned-Money-Tree, I see another little Karen, about age two. She is in a crib screaming for her/my dad. The Shaman comes to the crib and picks her up and then breaks the crib into pieces and throws them into a well or pit that suddenly appears. The wall behind the crib that he broke has a dark shadow on it.

She Fled Her Fears

This is the same area where the little girls were hiding under the dark, swampy leaves. The Shaman holds the toddler Karen as we walk to the other side, where Grandma is breast-feeding the infant and rocking the little Karen snatched from her cousin's sexual abuse. The rest of the little Karens are playing around Grandma. Again, the Shaman gives the toddler Karen to Grandma to soothe away the experience of abandonment, abuse, and powerlessness. As usual, with much gratitude, I thank all that is there, and leave—*wow!*

This was an amazing experience, and I easily understood the situation with that young child in the crib. When I was about two, my parents separated, and my dad took my mom and me to her mother's house. My first memory is being in a crib there, screaming for my dad to come back.

I continued to go to the Shaman, but for months nothing happened. I would walk the path, knock, and enter and then I would just lose focus, lose purpose. I kept trying, but I accepted that the dry spell was part of the process. And in early August 2012, it changed.

August 2012

This time, I see that the dark well/pit where the Shaman threw the crib has turned into a Reflecting Pool. When I look into it, a lovely man gazes back at me. I reach out and touch his cheek, and he does the same to me. After a moment, he comes out of the Reflecting Pool, and we follow the Shaman to the down-covered area where one learns patience. The man from the Reflecting Pool and I lie down together and make love. Then we get up, and we are in the right corner of the outside white space with the banyan tree. We are holding hands, and in the center of the space is a treasure chest of riches—ours. I recognize the man as my Other.

Also in late August of that year, I had a one-person show of *Broken Circle* at the University of Minnesota's Coffman Gallery. The publicity was great and resulted in newspaper and radio interviews as well as book sales. The opening coincided with the university's students returning to campus. The portraits were life-size, with the statements next to them. It was very powerful and satisfying to me, as I watched the gallery visitors walk from one piece to another, stopping to read and digest what each child's experience of their family's divorce had been. Again, I was blessed with a friend who did all the printing pro bono, he just wanted to be part of the team.

August 28, 2012

When I enter the space, my Shaman turns my clothes into fire! I am wearing flames! Then my flaming self moves to the water, where Clarity resides/floats, and

I become Passion—also riding on the water. Clarity and Passion are next to each other, floating on the blue water. They are about the same size. Clarity is brilliant white, and Passion is all orange, gold, and red flames. They are a constant presence, their easy soft movements in synch with the waves of the water they are riding.

In real life, I was having issues with my platelet count, so my acupuncturist focused treatment on my spleen.

Mid-September 2012

During the acupuncture treatment, I visit my Inner Shaman. When I enter, I see the room is filled with intense yellow light. In the middle there is a fountain spewing yellow light. The Shaman has me stand in the fountain to absorb the yellow light.

Later, the acupuncturist told me that yellow is spleen color in Chinese Medicine and also the color of the third Chakra.

Early November 2012

During a visit in November 2012, I approach the Shaman with my broken heart in my hands. The Shaman takes the pieces and places them in the Reflecting Pool. The water turns red and Other's face is obliterated. I feel much better now that my broken heart is there and not weighing me down by blocking or using my energy.

Late November 2012

During a later November visit, again I carry pieces of my broken heart in my hands—these accumulated over a two-year period of time. Again, the Shaman takes them and places them in the Reflecting Pool, and it turns red. He heaps the pieces into a pile and gives me a shovel. I scoop them up and throw them out into the swampy water that runs along the outside path. I understand that all the negative events, history, actions, and words that I have ever experienced in my life are deposited there in that swamp. Now all the broken-heart pieces are there too. Yes, the Reflecting Pool is inside, and yes, the swamp is outside, but as in dreams, things appear as needed, so I am inside and I am outside.

Then I drink a cup of green liquid and eat crushed red berries from the Creative Bush. The Shaman rubs the red berry juice on my face and body. We walk around, and I see that Clarity and Passion are quietly floating on their water.

During this time, I was regularly seeing a Jungian analyst. I shared my Inner Shaman journeys with him, and he was interested and supportive of me. I also decided to move to a larger apartment in a different part of the Twin Cities. I thought it would be good for me to live in an area where more artists live; I was looking for community.

Early December 2012

In early December, I go to the Shaman. We always walk left, first to the Creative Bush to eat the berries, then to see Grandma and the little Karens. Today, he takes me to the Reflecting Pool, and I vomit into it all my anger—the anger I was keeping in my right hip. Then he gives me the shovel again, and I shovel all the vomit in the Reflecting Pool into the swamp. When I am finished, my hip no longer hurts; when I look into the Reflecting Pool, a young me is gazing back. I am my Other.

I was still having platelet count issues, so my doctor sent me to a specialist for more hematology work. Hematology at Regions Hospital was located in the oncology department, and seeing that sign above the door gave me a moment of terror. They found nothing, but the count was getting too low, and the doctor mentioned a bone marrow transplant.

My new apartment bedroom was located under my landlady's bedroom; she snored so loudly that it consistently disturbed my sleep. When I mentioned the snoring and asked if she had a rug on her bedroom floor, she advised me that I should get earplugs. It was winter; things were getting ugly outside, and inside, I was sleep deprived and lonely. Things were not as I anticipated.

Late December 2012

I ask the Shaman to take my anxiety. I feel wrapped in anxiety, and it is penetrating every cell in my body. He proceeds to unwind this seeming barbed wire that is wound tightly around me. It takes a long time to unwind it all. Then he puts the anxiety wire into a cauldron, and it becomes molten metal. I lift the cauldron and pour the metal onto the down feathers. I don't know what else to do with it. The feathers absorb the molten metal.

She Didn't Recognize Her Self

Mid-January 2013

I flew to Santo Domingo, Dominican Republic, to photograph and interview some Domican young adults for my *Broken Circle* project. I had an assistant to help with all the technical details and ended up having a very successful five-day photo shoot. The plan was to have the pieces exhibited at a University in Santo Domingo in May during a conference about family, divorce, and children that was arranged by a family practice attorney in Santo Domingo.

March 2013

The Shaman takes me back to the dark corner place, and again I see the little Karen who was sexually abused for so long, still hiding under that leafy canopy. Behind her there is an infant—scared, unheld, unwelcome, un-everything infants need—and hungry, always hungry. I understand that these two are very important to connect with, but I have much work to do before they will respond. I understand that their wounds are primal, that they reappear so I will focus on their/my healing.

They have no trust. I crawl through the muck and mud so I can reach them. I pick up the infant, wrap her in a blanket, and begin to breast-feed her. I take the other little Karen by the hand, and we slowly walk around to show her where we live now. I tell her it isn't her fault; she is just like the other girls, not shameful, and she doesn't need to keep her secret anymore. She is hesitant, but I notice that the infant is contentedly nursing and actually gaining color—she is no longer the color of death. The Shaman leads me to Grandma, and she welcomes these two wounded Karens also. Grandma Klein is my source for healing, health, life; I bring these wounded parts of my Self to her for her sustenance.

I continued to photograph more kids for my *Broken Circle* project, as well as pursuing exhibition opportunities for my personal art work. Marketing took up a lot of time, but I realized that if I wanted to have my work seen, I needed to go through this process; no one was going to come knock at my door asking if I had any art to share! By April, there were hints that spring was going to really happen, and I always had a positive response to more light, longer days, and sunshine.

Mid-April 2013

I knock, and after I enter, the Shaman takes me to the Creative Bush and feeds me the berries and then puts some in my pocket. He takes money from the Money Tree and puts that in my pocket, too. We walk around to Grandma Klein, who is contentedly sitting in her rocker and breast-feeding infant Karen. The other little Karens are playing together and all seem happy here. I smile at Grandma, and we hug, a hug of deep love and gratitude. The Shaman and I walk on to the white outside door.

Standing outside is a little Karen who had been told, "That's for other people, not for us." That comment, as well as all the dashed hopes that would accompany such a negative statement, seemed to be the mantra for my family when I was little. Don't have expectations; don't always want. You're never satisfied.

Now the little one is standing in front of two people. I can see only their arms, as they are standing off to the side. In front of us is a vast land with tall green grasses. It was previously covered in white (perhaps snow?), but now grass covers the land as far as I can see. This little Karen starts walking through the grasses and gathering treasure from the vast green field. I turn around and see all the little Karens eating creative berries and drinking blue (related to communication, expression, and truth) liquid. Blue is the color of the throat chakra; perhaps the Shaman now gives us blue liquid to help us find our voices. The Shaman and I leave and walk past Clarity and Passion, who are slightly, softly moving, rocking on the water.

Mid-May 2013

I went to Santo Domingo, Dominican Republic, for the three-day conference that was developed around my *Broken Circle* project. It was held at UNIBE University. I had twenty of my images on exhibition, the text perfectly translated into Spanish, and the book available in

Spanish also. As the creator of the project, I was one of the scheduled speakers. A translator was available for me. I found it to be a satisfying experience to share my story of *Broken Circle*'s origins. I thought I'd be too shy or afraid to speak to the crowd, but I wasn't. Maybe that's why the Shaman gave us blue liquid! Many of the kids I had photographed in Santo Domingo came to the opening night, and it was incredibly rewarding to see their enthusiasm for the project, too.

Late May 2013

I approach with the infant Karen, and I am nursing her. After the usual walk around, I exit at the opening to the beach. Other is waiting for us; Other nurses the infant, and finally Other and I nurse each other. We sit down on the beach and hold the infant Karen and each other. Back inside, the color yellow, mixed with blue rain, showers me; it covers me as I walk. I see that the Colorful Sculpture is pulsing with very intense colors. When I am ready to leave, I thank my Shaman and open the door. I am aware that all aspects of the Shaman's residence are in me, including him, the colors, the symbols, the girls, the emotions, the relationships—

in *me*. It seems that I am beginning to know, allow, and

accept my Self. And I leave, walking along the path

back to a conscious awake state.

After much online research, I discovered that my blood pressure

medication was known to decrease platelet counts in some patients! So

I immediately made an appointment to discuss this with my doctor.

She changed my prescription, and it took over a year for my count to

return to normal.

I was not happy in my apartment and was thinking about another

move, this time perhaps to Florida. I had lived in Florida for about

fifteen years during my first marriage—so Florida, with its heat and

all its kitschy oddness, was not unknown to me. I felt ready to leave the

midwestern tundra and head south for the sunlight and beach; I just

didn't know yet in which part of Florida I wanted to live.

June 2013

I knock and say the password, and the Shaman opens the door. I immediately go to Grandma and take the infant Karen into my arms. Then I gather the little Karens, and we all walk back to the Creative Bush. The little Karens are integrated in me, and anything creative that I do involves them also, so feeding them from the Creative Bush is necessary. The Shaman feeds all of us the red berries and then gives us an orange liquid. After that fortification, we go out to the beach, and Other is waiting there. We all run and play. I come in to find the entwined Colorful Sculpture pulsing with energy, and I see all of us in the reflecting pool. The ceiling is open, with gold light, joy, abundance, and ease pouring in.

My son called to tell me that his wife had accepted a two-year overseas assignment, and in August, they were all moving from Sarasota, Florida, to Singapore; would I be interested in living in their house while they were gone? *Are you kidding?* So I gave notice on the rental apartment, contacted the movers, and the packing began.

Late July 2013

It is dark at the Shaman's, which is very unusual. I immediately notice that the beautiful golden light is missing. When I enter and it's dark, I don't know what to expect. There has always been a large dark smudge on the wall right near where Grandma sits. I always did my best to ignore it. Today, I walk up to confront the big, dark, towering form. I look up, knowing it is my Shadow—so much bigger than I am—hovering. It is moving. I am protecting the little girls by holding my arms out. I know I can't exorcise or extricate the shadow (like my broken heart), so I talk to it (her), and as I do, I grow taller, and Shadow shrinks in size. I tell her, "You are causing trouble; you are afraid." I knew Shadow ruled me too often, and when I confronted her, I immediately felt a physical sense of relief, of calming.

She Recognized Her Shadow

I flew to Sarasota on August 7, 2013, and the moving truck arrived three days later. Of course, I didn't know anyone there, but I had absolute confidence that Sarasota would be a good place for me. I was completely unaware of the spiritual community that exists in Sarasota, but as I discovered all of the classes and communities and circles and events, plus a fabulous book store, I knew this was a good place for me to land.

Late August 2013

I go to the Shaman, and I look like I do now—this age, this hair—instead of the younger version that had been visiting the Shaman. Once I am inside, we go to the Creative Bush and Money Tree. In my hands, I hold my art work, my photography. The Shaman takes it and feeds it to the roots of the Money Tree, and a golden column comes out of the earth and spirals around both the tree and the Creative Bush. At the top, it spreads open and soars upward, kind of like a sparkler. Then the Shaman takes the "sparkler," and it shrinks in size. He hands sparklers to all of us—Grandma, the little girls, and me. I see that the space outside is filled with more sparklers! When I look into the reflecting pool, all ages of me are gazing back—integrated in me.

Early November 2013

I walk the path, knock, and say the words. The Shaman opens the door and puts his hands on my shoulders. I tell him I am so anxious. It seems the more anxiety I acknowledge, the more I discover. Not a surprise, as I seem to have lived a long time without connecting to my real emotions, and now I've tapped into a deep well. Again, he takes me to the little girls in the middle of his space. They are playing, and he puts me into the middle of them. They circle around me—I keep growing tall, then shrinking to their height, up and down as they circle around me singing "You Are My Sunshine." They think this is very funny, and in my dizziness, I do too! Then I go out to the beach, and Other is there. He puts his hands on my shoulders, looks into my eyes, and says, "I believe in you. I love you." I go back inside and walk with the Shaman to a wall near the entrance door, and we stop in front of it. It turns indigo (intuition, ideas, dreams, ambitions, goals, inner strength, and self image) and is like a mirror; everything reflected is of that color. I step into the wall, and the indigo

color bathes and enters me as healing energy. I leave the

Indigo Mirror wall and walk to the Reflecting Pool; I

gaze into it and see all the little Karens are in me, and

Other is there, too.

I feel overwhelmed with waves of crippling anxiety. Of course, the

doctor I went to immediately gave me a perscription for that anxiety,

and guess what? It worked! Unfortunately, it was addictive, so I knew

I would have to find another way to deal with this problem. I was

now living in a large house in a gated community in a city inhabited

by tourists. I often went to the beach and began to photograph there.

I was still marketing my *Broken Circle* project. But I did not know my

way around the city, and the increasingly heavy tourist traffic was

becoming a problem for me. However, I just kept on keeping on. I

signed up for yoga classes and found someone to deal with my curly hair,

which was responding capriciously to the humidity. I started attending

a nearby church. It was the current version of the denomination my

great-grandpa/Inner Shaman was part of, and I felt comfortable there—

not inspired but comfortable. And, it was a good opportunity to meet

people, which I did. I met my new best friend, Julie. We each had three children, were both single now, and were newly arrived in Sarasota and looking to find our Spiritual Paths.

November 16, 2013

I am still feeling very anxious when I go to the Shaman. I tell him I am alone, lonely, and isolated. I give him all my anxieties again. I hold out my hands; they are full of little dark stones. He takes all of the stones and deposits them in a little black bag, then feeds them to the roots of the Creative Bush.

November 18, 2013

For the first time ever, today we walk to the right, not the left! I am aware that in many traditions, the left side represents feminine/receiving and the right represents masculine/giving. Our first stop is at the Indigo Mirror. I am still inside the mirror, and my Shaman has me tap on my third eye to remind myself to trust my intuition. I understand that a lot of my stress is in knowing and not accepting—intuition and ego. We walk around, and I see that the tall beautiful, pulsing Colorful Sculpture is not visible as usual. There is a transparent dark shade pulled down in front of it. When I walk to the beach, I take the infant from Other, and he walks to the ocean and sits down. I go back inside and see that everything else is the same, and once again, I give the infant to Grandma. I sit on the bench with her, and the infant and little Karens are around us, busily talking, playing, reading, and making shadow puppets on the wall.

Late in November, I go again. Everything seems the same, and I see that Other is walking down the beach. Clarity and Passion are both very present—larger and moving rapidly on the water.

I had an appointment for a massage, and when I entered the spa, I glanced through the door on the right and saw two women sitting across a table with a deck of cards between then. I asked the receptionist if they were doing tarot readings, and she said that they had just started to offer them. So of course I had to schedule a reading after my massage. That was when I met a woman who became a dear friend. She had a career as a psychotherapist before she retired to Sarasota about ten years ago. Now she was writing poetry, making jewelry, and doing Reiki healing. She was very interested in and supportive of my photography. Often, she would call to inquire what I was working on. She took me to my first Shamanic Journey, itself a wonderful and scary adventure, where I was first introduced to the spirit guides; my first guide was a fox.

December 14, 2013

I go to the Shaman with a hurt heart in my hand. He takes it and goes outside the front door. On the left side, where the dark water is, I see an alligator, and he feeds my hurt heart to the alligator. I understand I have been given the gift of lying—this is not clear to me yet, but I believe lying and fear are strong presences in me. Because of the chaos in my early family, I was always reading the weather and responding to the way the winds were blowing. The sexual abuse made me able to totally separate from my Self. I had no personal authenticity, as a result of those experiences but was able to survive by lying.

I am bound in a rusty barbed wire that represents my lies. My Shaman takes the end of the barbed wire and begins to pull it as I slowly spin around. It unwinds my lies. When I was growing up, barbed wire was a presence in the farm's pastures; sometimes it was electrically charged. I was often shocked because I touched it; it looked benign, and I wouldn't know for sure if it was charged unless I touched it.

We walk to the Creative Bush and Money Tree, and they reach out to spin me around so I can escape the wire. I am standing in front of Shadow, and some of my spirit guides join me—owl, fox, frog, and alligator. They all, except Shadow, help to spin me around. We all walk with the Shaman to Grandma, who is in the rocker with little Karen and the infant. I sit down by her and cry; I cry really hard. I feel I hurt them by lying. I see that I hurt my work by not being of true heart. I go to the little girls, and they help spin me around, still unwinding the wire of lies from me. Clarity and Passion also help spin me out of the wire, and then I walk out to the beach. Other is leaning against the wall, and I tell him to leave. The big Colorful Sculpture is still hidden by the dark shade that's been pulled over it. Back inside, I go to the Indigo Mirror, finally free of the lie wire. I feel as if integration has happened and going forward with a clear heart is possible.

My entire family came to Florida for Christmas and my big 7-0 birthday. It was wonderful, and I was filled with joy. All the restaurants we went to were good, the beach was perfect, and everyone was in good spirits. And I didn't mind being my age, for a change.

January 3, 2014

I see that Shadow has changed; the letters "RIP" are faint on the wall where the smudge used to be. The mound of down in the middle of the space has been replaced by a large tub of water, and I am suddenly floating in Wisdom Water. The sexually abused little Karen has a name, Karen Aphrodite, and she is cautiously integrating with the rest of the Karens. There is now a black shroud over the Colorful Sculpture. Other is sitting outside by the water, letting the tides wash over him.

January 6, 2014

The Colorful Sculpture has disintegrated; all the colors are lying on the ground. All that remains is the armature, and it is very faded and weak. No more pulsing of the energies that were housed in this large, beautiful sculpture. I watch the colors drop to the ground and sprout into little flowers.

January 8, 2014

I am clothed all in black, mourning. Grandma takes the little girls to bake cookies, and I go to the white space where now my work is hung, and it has turned into a studio! Finally, I have a studio! I start to work on a new piece depicting lies/love, hurt/humor, etc. When I see Clarity and Passion, I am between them, but now I am not in black mourning clothes; I am naked. I take the infant Karen out to the beach, and I see that Other is still leaning against the wall. I turn around and go back inside to where the Colorful Sculpture disassembled. I pick up the colored pieces/flowers and put them in a basket. I see that the armature of the original piece still remains. I take the basket full of the colors to the Indigo Mirror. I walk back to the Shaman with my sadness, disappointment, hurt, loneliness, and anxiety and put all of them together, along with my black clothes, and I give the bundle to him. He turns around and feeds it to the Creative Bush by laying it at the roots so it will be absorbed and something new will come of that dark. Alchemy indeed.

I am well aware that since my family was here, and is now gone, I am experiencing an aloneness, a loneliness that is very difficult for me. I feel isolated and not sure where to turn. This manifests in sleeplessness, worry, fear, and overwhelming stress.

She Waited Within

January 18, 2014

Today there is a new, large empty space next to the Money Tree. I understand that it is becoming an Imaginarium. I have the basket with the colors/flowers from the now-deconstructed sculpture, and I empty the basket on the ground in front of the Imaginarium. The colors/flowers spread out and become a Magic Carpet at the entrance. I don't step on it but turn around and walk to the beach. Other is there; we are lying on the beach on top of each other, and the waves are gently lapping. He is also still leaning against the wall.

I find someone who teaches meditation and sign up. I go to painting classes, part of my art therapy plan. I go to acupuncture to help relieve stress and sleeplessness. And I am beginning to understand and accept how alone I feel in this large house in this city where I have no family and am just beginning to make friends.

January 20, 2014

This visit, I step on the Imaginarium's Magic Carpet, and it envelops me—I become covered in the colors; they swirl around me. While covered in the colors, I begin to swirl around and spin right up to the cosmic universe; I am like a tornado rotating while sheathed in the colors. It is not at all scary, and I understand the Imaginarium exists to recharge my imagination. I go directly to Other, who is still standing by the entrance to the beach. I open my mouth to talk, and all the lies I had absorbed spew out, like vomit. But it was words; I covered him in words. Then I see the two of us lying on the beach, and we are taken out to sea—washed out to sea by the waves, as if returned to the Mother.

January 22, 2014

My Shaman tells me to call my doctor regarding my confusion about my medications—to seek additional information. Periodically, everything seems overwhelming. I am looking for a new doctor; I tend to have doubt about doctors' conclusions and perscriptions. Then, one by one, Shaman helps me take my fear, anxiety, and uncertainty and put them—all of them—in a bag. It does seem that the more I address the anxiety, the more I name my fears through Shaman visits or my self-care regimen, the more manageable the fears and anxiety become; they are not gone but become manageable. My animal totems come and carry

the bag to the studio! The one fear remaining inside of
me—loneliness—I take out, and Alligator picks it up
and takes it to the studio too. Today when I leave, I feel
calm, relieved, and stronger.

I meet more women who become really good friends, and I continue
to explore Sarasota's spiritual community. I attend the new and full
moon women's meditation group. I also now have a gallery representing
my Siesta Key photography. Faithfully, I go to yoga classes and have
acupuncture, and I find a new doctor who doesn't over-prescribe and a
dentist who takes my insurance.

February 1, 2014

On this visit, there is now a Wishing Well past the door
to the beach. So I drop my wishes into the well, for me,
my family, the planet.

The Sarasota traffic is horrific when all the snowbirds are here. The
highways weren't built to accommodate all the large cars and SUVs.
I became more and more anxious about driving, even to the grocery

store. Sometimes I just had to call a cab to get where I needed to go. Otherwise, I just stayed at home rather than drive. That anxiety grew into a panic attack, and I was transported by ambulance to the emergency room, sure that I was having a heart attack. Everything checked out; I did not have a cardiac incident. But the panic attack was very real and scary. I also bought a larger car to help alleviate the driving anxiety. My little Prius did not make me feel secure on the highways.

Febrary 14, 2014

Today, I again tell the Shaman about my anxiety, as it seems out of control. He takes me to the beach doorway and gives the end of the barbed wire around my neck to Other. It feels as if I am controlled by my anxieties and fears—being wrapped in barbed wire is a good analogy for my paralysis. Then Shaman spins me around counterclockwise, and we all walk to the left, past Charity and Passion, past the studio, past Grandma and the little girls and totems, all of whom are helping to spin me so the anxiety wire unwinds from my neck. They keep going until I am in front of the Indigo

Mirror. Suddenly the wire is on fire, and it becomes molten metal. The molten metal becomes a sculpture, a large knotted ball that the Shaman places with me in the Indigo Mirror for healing.

I have two more panic attacks and get sent to a cardiologist to ascertain that my heart is not the problem. I end up having a heart monitor implanted into my chest to record any incidents. To date there have been none; again, gratitude. While it is reassuring that I'm healthy, the stress seems bigger than I can manage. When I take it to the Shaman, he always does something to alleviate it, yet it is so ingrained that it keeps recurring.

April 2, 2014

First to the Creative Bush and Money Tree, pass through the Imaginarium, then to where RIP Shadow lives on the wall. In front of Shadow, the Shaman creates a fire and tells me to enter the fire to burn out my fears—a Fear Fire! I think of my fears as I enter the fire—so numerous: driving, being alone, getting lost, eating, loneliness, my work, health, money, age, where I will live? Then we go to Grandma, who is still rocking the little Karen and nursing the infant Karen. I talk to her about feeling not integrated, not rooted, and I tell her that I think it is because of my daddy leaving and separating from us, but she said she thinks the cause for those feelings is the sexual abuse. I walk past the studio where the little girls are happily painting, singing, and creating. Then I walk past Clarity and Passion. At the opening to the beach, I find Other, and we walk, hand in hand, down the beach. We are also lying at the water's edge with the waves lapping over us; the great Mother is caressing us. Then I walk to the Wishing Well and set my intentions—to live my life with courage and confidence; to have my live-in studio space; to have a steady money stream with my work; that my *Broken Circle* book continues to sell and expand internationally. I am healthy and grateful; I sleep well, eat well, and practice yoga, meditation, and prayer. Then we walk to the Indigo Mirror, and I place two of my friends who are not well into it for healing energies, for their improved health.

I have long noticed that I do not have productive visits to the Shaman if there are other people around. I can always go there, but I don't receive the gifts, and the insights may not happen. I know the hiatus is temporary. I am exploring more spiritual avenues and opportunities to learn, including Reiki training.

April 28, 2014

At the Shaman's, I go to the beach door, and Other is there. I tell him to leave, as he is too much a distraction for me now. Other picks us up from the water's edge and walks down the beach, still holding us. He turns around and collapses to his knees and screams. Then he turns into a long, dark snake and slithers into the ocean. Such drama. I come back inside, and all the little Karens join me in the pool in the center of the Shaman's space. Apparently the down feathers have turned into a large pool of Wisdom Water again.

May 12, 2014

The smudge on the wall that morphed into the RIP Shadow after my first confrontation with her sometimes gets very large, looming over everyone and causing great anxiety and fear. I have been able to tell her to stop it to get her to settle down. Now, though, I decide to incorporate Shadow—I invite her to come down off the wall. I tell her that I don't want her to be separate and not included anymore. I apologize for hating her, fearing her, and excluding her. I can see she doesn't trust me, but she chooses to leave the wall after I assure her that she can be happy, too.

As she leaves the wall, the big dark smudge turns into a little one-inch square, gray in color. Then little stick legs grow out of the bottom two corners of the square! And on her little stick legs are silver pointy-toed slippers. She readily joins the other little Karens. Although she is unique looking, they welcome her and seem to not notice her "uniqueness." We are into diversity here!

May 17, 2014

Today the Shaman takes me to a tree. It is in front of where smudge/RIP Shadow used to be on the wall. The tree has banyan roots at the trunk, a middle of weeping willow, and the top is a royal palm. He places me and the little Karens into the base of the tree, and the banyan roots wrap around us. I understand that this is the Truth Tree.

My son and his family are here from Singapore for a too-brief stay, and two of my granddaughters visit also. I do so much better with the family around, yet I know it is temporary, as vacations always are. During this time, I receive word that my friend who introduced me to Shamanic Journeys and many other parts of Sarasota's spiritual community has commited suicide. While I was very saddened at this news, I also respected her decision. I knew I would miss her terribly, yet I had no real knowledge of what may have propelled her to this decision.

July 18, 2014

I am thrilled to see that today Passion and Clarity are joined by Louise Nevelson! She is clothed in black, of course, and wearing the omnipresent black eye makeup, but what a greater reminder about following one's art passion!

How I had pored over Louise Nevelson's books—admiring images of her large sculptures and reading about her life as an artist. The demands, the creativity—nothing stood in her way.

August 14, 2014

The Shaman takes me to the Creative Bush, where he wraps my first and second chakras in red and orange colors. Then he takes me to the Fear Fire to burn out guilt, fear, and shame so I can accept abundance. Guilt—not deserving, not good enough, not competent; shame at wanting and not feeling that I deserve, not standing my ground—perfect fodder for all that anxiety.

Then he cuts me open and plants seeds of courage and confidence in me that will grow in every cell of my body. Out to the beach and I see the snake slowly swimming back and forth. I watch him, and I walk into the water, dive in, and have my way with him.

I have started to paint a lot now. I really have no training in painting, which is why I can do it freely, without expectation of results. And I find it very satisfying. I paint my anxiety, numerous times.

September 1, 2014

Other is no longer a snake swimming back and forth; he is standing on the shore. We are happy to see each other and hug, as always. I think Other is my animus, and the struggles I have in myself manifest in his presence. Inside, I walk to the Wishing Well and put in my wishes for myself, my family, the world—may we be loved, may we be healthy, may we be safe, may we be happy. I look up and see that there is now a large copper sconce on the wall next to the Wishing Well. I understand that this is where the universe gives me abundance, and there is a little pig sitting on the floor in front of it. Her name is Polly, and she is a spirit guide that helps to manifest abundance. I continue walking and see that, where the Colorful Sculpture used to be, there is now a Void. It is a large space, a Void that is inhabited by colors and energies, Reiki, spirits, guides, archangels, and ascended masters. I walk into the space that is both so welcoming and visually not there—it is a Void, yet all of those energies are thriving there.

She Knew Why but Not When

September 2, 2014

Today, the Creative Bush and the Money Tree are in a swirl of copper snow. On the other side of the Imaginarium, there is a Worry Web, and I am in the middle of it. It completely surrounds me. My parents both appear and start to unravel the Web—a very slow, tedious process, as it has been so many years in the making. They remove a strand at a time and place them in the Fear Fire. I am grateful for their help. But as they toil away, a bunch of little Karens drop out of the Web; they are all very pale and dressed in white. I know these little ones were stunted by worries that my parents taught me. I take the worry girls to Grandma Klein, and she cares for them. Outside on the beach, since Other is no longer a snake, he is waiting for me, and when I approach, our cells meld. Now there is a form that looks like my black-and-white handmade paper art that is us. It is solid and static. Inside, in the Void with the many colors and energies, I enter that space. I linger there as

the energies permeate me. Then I go on to the Indigo
Mirror for healing.

It's early fall in Sarasota, which means the snowbirds are still up north,
the traffic is much lighter, and my stress about driving is less. I found
a therapist who did EMDR, a technique designed to reduce the long-
lasting effects of distressing memories by developing more adaptive
coping mechanisms, who helped me to overcome my driving fear.

September 19, 2014

At the beach, Other is waiting, and again I tell him to
leave. A large black hawk swoops down, grabs him by
the shoulders, and carries him out over the water. He
is dangling—the hawk's talons gripping his shoulders.
I wince at the thought of that pain. Then the material
that enveloped us as our cells merged becomes ashes on
the ground. It seems there is always a love/hate struggle
between us. I scoop the ashes in my hands, and the
Shaman gives me a box to put them in. I fill it and leave
the box on the beach. I go back inside, and the little

Karens are singing "I Can See Clearly Now." Absolutely uplifting!

September 21, 2014

Today in the Fear Fire, I burn out my delusions. Most of them burn rapidly, and there is just a small core left. I ask for help to pull it out and then receive the instruction to "let it go." I did, and it fell out. I release the Root of Delusion, and, after it falls out, I pick it up and carry it out to the beach and then place it in the box of ashes.

I think my new body of work with the reflections is about delusion. I regularly attend a Spiritual Awakening class and learn about spirits, guides, manifesting, and setting intentions—so much I didn't know anything about!

October 3, 2014

At the beach, the bird of prey flies toward me with Other still dangling by the shoulders; suddenly, it releases Other from its talons. He lands on the shore. I walk toward him and realize he is but a shell of himself. He is like one of those helium baloons! My Shaman approaches and actually kicks the Other/shell, and it deflates. That, too, gets put into the box with the ashes and my Root of Delusion. Did I want Other to have my answers?

October 7, 2014

The little Karens are in a busy state; there is much activity in the studio, which is a good sign! I walk past Clarity, Louise Nevelson, and Passion to the beach door, and as I approach, I see a man leaning against the wall. Of course I think it is Other, but he is wearing khaki clothes. I approach and see it is my dad! We have a lengthy conversation that is the first time I am able to tell him about feeling abandoned so many years ago, about the sexual abuse, about my insecurities in relationships and self-esteem, and about my fears. He hugs me and tells me how sorry he is. I bring him in to sit on the bench next to Grandma. They don't seem surprised to see each other, and the little Karen that was rescued from the crib, the one Grandma has been rocking and playing with, now goes to my dad. He lifts her up on his lap. He looks about the age he was when all the heartbreak and fear was happening to that child. They become totally involved with each other.

She Had That Dream Again

The church I was attending decided to have an art gallery space, and I was the first artist asked to exhibit. Needless to say, I was very happy about this and started to get my new beach exploration photography matted and framed. I also created a catalogue to accompany the exhibit.

November 1, 2014

Today, the usual knock, password, door opens, and greeting of smile and the Shaman's hands on my shoulders. Then we go directly to the Truth Tree, where I again set my intentions: for my work, for my health, for my abundance. Then we walk to the bench where my dad is, to my grandma, and to my mom. Then we walk past the open studio space where much activity is going on, past Clarity and Passion to the opening to the beach. At the beach, I dive into the water and swim out to a pod of dolphins surrounding a whale. I know the whale's name is Sho and one of the dolphins is Ronin. The whale swims under me, and I lie on her back. I can feel her heart beating with mine. It is very soothing and peaceful to recline on her. I stay there for a while, and then I am back inside walking with my Shaman to the Wishing Well, where I repeat the words "May all beings be happy, may all beings be loved, may all beings be safe, may all beings be well." We then proceed to the place of Abundance. Polly the Pig sits in front of the large Abundance Sconce on the wall; she is the spirit guide. I accept; I allow abundance in my health, friendships, love, finances, and creativity. Then we proceed to the Void, where there are only color and energy vibrations; I immerse myself there and become charged with the energies from the guides and spirits, the archangels, and the ancestors. Then on to the Indigo Mirror, almost always the last stop at the Shaman's before I leave. It was a very calming visit today.

I went to Minnesota for Thanksgiving and to visit with my daughter-in-law's mother, who had been diagnosed with pancreatic cancer. The day I arrived, I went to see her, and after our visit, she asked me to come to her room; she wanted to show me something. It was her altar, and it had a framed picture of Mary on it. She told me she knew that Mary was with her now and that she could smell the scent of roses when Mary came. She and her husband had been involved in Unity for years, and now her Unity beliefs brought her a quiet grace in her transition. She had an unexpectedly rapid decline, and I opted to stay in Minnesota longer because I thought I could be helpful. I wasn't sure what that meant, but intuitively, I knew that I needed to stay. She had been a Reiki healer for many years, and since I had become involved in Reiki, I knew I could bring her some ease. I witnessed an amazing session with an energy worker from hospice who came to help with her transition. At her beautiful service, a life well-lived was memorialized. I felt blessed to be present. Upon returning to Florida, I felt enlightened, changed, and grateful for the experience that I had witnessed. It was right before Christmas when I returned, and I immediately connected with my friends for support, solace, and conversation.

Recent visits to the Inner Shaman have been very quiet, possibly because much of the healing I sought has taken place. I do always get more Creative Bush berries and feed my latest ideas to the Money Tree, and sometimes to the Imaginarium and the Truth Tree as well, but usually I just don't stay. It is all very quiet there now. I have found the activity to be a bit cyclical. When I have greater need, there's more activity, and when it's quieter, I seem more grounded.

March 4, 2015

I walk to the door, knock, repeat the password, and there he is; we are always happy to see each other. He leads me to the Creative Bush, and I get fed the red berries. I am working on a new gallery project, and the Shaman takes it and feeds it to the Money Tree. The Money Tree area is now shimmering with a fine copper glow. Then, at the Imaginarium, I step on the Magic Carpet and am swirled up and into sources to recharge my imagination. Then to the Truth Tree—I sit in the tree, and the little girls join me, as do all the totems! This is new. Usually I sit there and list my intentions, sometimes struggling to make sure I am using the right words. But today, after we all gather there, I lead all of them on a dive down through the roots of the Truth Tree, into Earth. Shaman didn't come, but the little girls and the totems are diving with me. That means there is a diving pig, fox, owl, alligator, frog, and crow along with a multitude of little Karens. We are diving through the color red, and it seems to take quite a while.

Finally we glimpse the destination of our dive. We are at the center of the Earth Mother. There is a glowing, pulsating white core that welcomes us. We all dive into the white, and it is beyond beauty, peace, joy—it is the source of all that nurtures us. When it is time to leave, I lead the dive up and out the other side of Earth. Again it is through the color red, and we eventually come out on the other side of the Earth, then into the heavens, arcing around back to where we started. We enter through my crown chakra and are back with the Inner Shaman. After re-entry, we all go out to the beach and rest. I eventually continue my walk, stopping at the Wishing Well for the prayers for me, my family, and the world, and at the Sconce of Abundance, I allow and accept abundance. At the Void, where the colors and energies await me, I enter and am embraced and surrounded. That leaves a stop at the Indigo Mirror, and my visit is complete. I thank my Shaman, and we nod and smile at each other.

I've started to see a new Energy Worker/Therapist. I attended a spiritual memoir workshop at the church and started to write—first a paragraph, then a page—about my Inner Shaman. I had been keeping a journal of my daily experiences, and I included the shamanic visits. That meant I had to plow through all that writing to find my Inner Shaman entries. But I felt it was very important to document my experience.

March 21, 2015

At 4 a.m., I awoke—thin spacetime. I have been thinking a lot about my parents—mostly my mom and the fears she planted in me. With that on my mind, I went to my Inner Shaman to tell him I needed to deal with my fears—again. The Fear Web that my parents dismantled was very helpful, but I still have residue that restricts me. He leads me first to the Creative Bush, and I eat the berries. My hands become full of my paintings, and I give them to the Money Tree, at the root so it will absorb them. Then I go to the Imaginarium, and, as I swirl upward, wrapped in the colors, I become full of painting ideas—new pieces, large abstract pieces using the colors representative of emotions. There is a lot of vibrant energy in the work I am seeing. Then on to the Fear Fire. The Shaman places me in the flames, and again my fears burn out of me; they turn into black discs that move upward and turn into smoke as they hit the air. Then I go to the Truth Tree, and my intentions are very spontaneous, and I begin listing my fears: fear of being happy, fear of adventure, fear of making decisions, of joy, love, success, money, praise, success, physical weakness, being alone, driving, being lost, crowds, interstates, being smart, eating, being dumb, indecision, earning responsibilities, sickness, accidents, swimming, dancing, singing, choking, commitment, failure … the list went on for a long time.

After the naming, I leave the Truth Tree, and we walk past where my dad and my grandma sit. They are very faded now, not the vibrant people they were, but they still have a presence. However, my mom is still sitting there, not faded. I sit down next to her and tell her how difficult it is for me to have all the fears she/they gave me—how growing up, I didn't receive the messages from her that I needed: that I was loved or capable or special or smart or creative or anything else positive. Instead, I heard that I was never satisfied, that it was hell on Earth, that I had a big mouth, that I would be sorry one day. I explain to her that the chaotic environment that was my home didn't give me a good foundation from which to grow, and I, at age seventy-two, am still struggling with this.

My mom stands up and motions for me to do the same. Then she puts her mouth on mine and inhales very long and deep. She breathes in the fears she had given me and then turns her head and exhales them in a stream of fog. I watch the fears turn into little Karens. They are all pale and sickly looking, of various sizes and ages. They gather around us, their blue eyes looking up to me. I am overwhelmed. I don't walk any farther; I have to leave. A thank you and I left; I had to write it down!

She, We and Me

My son was in the States on business and managed to visit me in Sarasota for a few days. I was so happy to see him; I arranged for all my friends to meet me for lunch so they could meet him. I loved having him around, albeit for a brief visit. I have become aware how stressful it has been for me to be living in my son's house without all my "stuff." That is their can opener, their plates, their couch, their plants, etc. I didn't realize how adrift I felt, even though the house and space and environment are beautiful and safe; I didn't have my things around me to anchor me. This was a huge insight.

March 20, 2015

I go to the Inner Shaman knowing I will have to do something with the newly arrived little Fear Karens. They are patiently waiting for me, and I decide to gather all of the little girls—the healthier Karens and the Fear Karens—and Shadow and take them outside to the beach. I tell them to take off their clothes and play in the water and on the beach, that they need some Vitamin D, and after they get some sun they will all feel better, and I will decide what to do next. Then I leave.

March 27, 2015

Today, I take all the little girls to the Void, where the energies and colors reside along with the archangels, guides, and ancestors. I believe the little ones' healing can happen here, or at least begin here.

March 30, 2015

I am aware that I am not sure what to do with these little Fear Karens. My grandma is very faded, so I can't go to her, as I've done previously with the other little Karens. But I go to the Void, and one little fear Karen comes to me. She is the one who is physical fear. I quickly realize that physical fear is one of my major fears; many of the other ones are branches of that: fear of driving, fear of choking, fear of being alone, fear of getting up in the night, fear of swimming, fear of aging, etc. Anyway, I walk around the Shaman's space, trying to figure out who could help me, and nothing seems right till I get to my grandma's rocking chair. She is not completely gone, but she is so faded. I intuitively sit down and hold the little one on my lap. My Shaman comes to us with a cup of yellow liquid and gives it to the child. I do what I saw my grandma do—rock and cuddle the child, reassure her, and make shadow puppets on the wall.

I understood that all of these fears grew out of my mother's constant warning that "something" could happen, and that "something" would not be winning the lottery! I could not take swimming lessons because I might drown. No camps for me; something might happen. My mother did lose her first husband to cancer and her dad did have a stroke early in his life. She had held an elected political office, then married my dad and ended up living on a farm with her in-laws. Her life was not one of joy and adventure. She concluded from all this that life was hell on earth and routinely shared that perspective with me.

April 3, 2015

Today, the little Karens are all mingled together. First, we go to the Imaginarium and swirl around in the colors as we spiral up, up. This is a very energizing experience. After that, we walk to the Truth Tree: *The power of God is in me, the grace of God surrounds me. I am here and I am safe.* Then we continue walking around; some choose to go to the studio, and some continue walking with me. We go past the beach and don't go out; we make wishes at the Wishing Well for love, joy, peace, and safety for all. At Abundance, we accept and allow abundance for our efforts to generate our money stream. Then at the Void, a whole lot of the ones who reside there come out and follow us to the area where there is nothing now— but was once the dank swampy area where the first two little Karens were dragged out of the muck. This is also where infant Karen's crib had been, the crib that the Shaman destroyed. In this area, where these two dark events happened, we all gather and watch and wait. Yes, it is Good Friday today.

Poor sleep last night; is Blood Moon energy keeping me awake? I had been listening to numerous presenters from Hay House, and I signed up for a few Webinars that I found interesing. Tools, I am gathering tools to keep me focused, balanced, and able to sleep.

April 8, 2015

I went to the Inner Shaman, and he took my handmade paper pieces and fed them to roots of the Creative Bush. Then, at the Money Tree, he gave my photographs, books, and paintings to the roots. He then took me to the Imaginarium to swirl in the colors, then to Clarity to absorb me, then to Abundance. That seems like a holy trinity—Money Tree, Clarity, Abundance! Abundance has been that copper-colored sconce on the wall but now is morphing into something else. I cannot yet describe it, but it is evolving now!

April 11, 2015

On the next visit, everything is as usual on our walk until we get to the opening that leads to the beach. At the opening, there now appears a statue of Selket the Egyptian goddess, with her arms outstretched and a scorpion as part of her headdress. Usually she is seen protecting Tutankhamun's shrine. She is facing in toward the large space, her outstretched arms offering protection.

In my real world, we decided to sell our Minnesota house. Since my son and his family will be back in Sarasota on July 1, I looked for a new rental place in Sarasota. I knew where I didn't want to live, so that helped narrow the choices.

April 14, 2015

I knock on the door, and the Shaman opens it, smiles, and takes my hand to lead me to the Creative Bush and then to the Money Tree. I step on the Magic Carpet of the Imaginarium, and the colors swirl around me, and up I go. This is always exhilirating, freeing. I have no sense of "landing" or coming out of the Imaginarium; I just go on to the next thing. In this instance, we next go to the rocker, where now there is just a shadow of Grandma Klein. I gather all the little Karens around. I see their ages are varied; the oldest is maybe eight. The Fear Karens still look pale but seem to be integrating.

Shadow has maintained her unique identity, is fully integrated, and participates with the others. Perhaps she will be able to help the Fears. She seems more eager; once she was off the wall and those little stick legs and slippers popped out, she was good to go. The Fear Karens are not so robust, yet. But they are mingling now. I talk to all of them, encourage them to spend the day finding their happiness: create in the studio, go out and play on the beach. But first, we join the waiting spirits and guides, archangels, the ancestors, the Reiki colors and energies, Sophia, and Jesus at the dank swampy area where the first two little Karens were dragged out of the muck; where the little Karen's crib had been until the Shaman destroyed it. There, at that dark place, now grows a thousand-blossom lotus flower! It is huge, brilliant white, shimmering, and beautiful, growing out of the mucky swamp. And sitting in front of it is Polly the Pig. We all stand in awe, and then the little ones approach it. Each takes a petal and eats it.

I have more days of feeling grounded.

April 15, 2015

A most unusual experience this visit. The Shaman immediately leads me to the middle of the space. I lie there and watch myself elevate. It is indeed scary, but I need to do it. As I leave my body, I look down, and I see the entire Shaman space from above. All of the pieces are in place, and I see shimmers from the light bouncing off them. I realize that it is my Self that I am looking at from this elevated place.

Early May

When I went this time, the Shaman had gathered up all the broken heart pieces that I'd brought to him over the past years, and they turned into a large, beautiful golden egg-shaped light that he put into my chest.

Awaiting Eros

I have incorporated a sitting meditation every morning, which has become very important to my sense of self. I've been having a lot of prayers answered—the apartment that I wanted, a New York art dealer wanting my work, my early-morning bike ride meditations—this is a lot of good stuff. This morning, on a beach walk, I realized the joy I'd like to be experiencing is always shaded by the "shit storm" of negatives that keep popping up in my mind: the other shoe's going to drop, that's not for us, you're never satisfied, you always want more, etc. Of course, my German lineage on both sides doesn't give a lot of permission for joy!

May 23, 2015

I took this insight to the Inner Shaman. He welcomed me with a box, like a big moving box, and invited me to put/throw those negatives into the box. As they pop up at any time, the box is available 24/7. In the middle of all that "shit storm," he showed me a seed. It was a seed of Joy. He took the infant Karen and put her in the middle of his space, and he gathered all the little Karens, Grandma Klein, and my parents. He planted the Joy seed in the infant Karen, and as it sprouts and grows, it will manifest in the rest of the Karens of all ages! That means me, too!! I have been doing a bike ride every morning, before the heat gets too intense. I ride around the neighborhood for about forty-five minutes, and I am finding that, not only do I look forward to the exercise, but it's very meditative too. On a ride this week, a crow was flying next to me at shoulder height. He flew along as I pedaled and then perched on a mailbox. A few feet farther down the road was a large turtle—at least twelve or fourteen inches across. And it was walking along, observing the environment, its little head turning from side to side. When I got home, I had to look those two up in my Spirit Guides book. Yes, crow, I'm on the verge of manifesting something I've been working toward for a while. And, yes turtle, I will take time to nurture myself and observe and feel my emotions.

I have also started to attend a Monday night mindfulness meditation group that is led by a monk from Sri Lanka. My mind experiences forty-fve minutes of peace.

Early June 2015

My Shaman takes me by the hand, and we walk. The space is quiet. He points out what I have available to me: he starts with the Creative Bush—creativity, then the Imaginarium—imagination. He stops at every place and points out what I have: Truth, Comfort, Support, Love, Space, Clarity, Passion, Beauty, Protection, Hope, Spirituality, Abundance, Wisdom, Intuition.

And I realize that I don't need to frantically continue my external search. My Inner Shaman has awakened me to my Self. I can accept and allow my Self to be; just like the Universe planned it!

The past two years have been an amazing and unexpected adventure for me on my path. My Inner Shaman visits ground me; they enlighten, comfort, and heal me. The strong spiritual community in Sarasota also impacts me in a very profound way. Usually, I visit the Inner Shaman very early in the morning. The environment there is much quieter now, but I still go, and he leads me around the beautiful space to remind me of all the facets of my Self, the powerful gifts and talents I possess within, and the ancestors and guardians who travel with me. And so it is.

Karl Emil Otto

Clara Otto Klein

Karen Klein

Karen Klein is a seeker and a photographer/visual artist from Sarasota, Florida. She has an MFA in Studio Arts Photography from the University of Minnesota. In 2006, Klein came back to making her art after years in the corporate environment.

She combined her film and digital imagery to create a visual narrative that explored the intersection of dream, desire, and memory in an emotive form of visual storytelling, drawing from a collection of iconic images to create new perspectives in which her stories unfold. Work from the *In Focus, Out of Memory* portfolio is included in this book.

In her recent work, *Key Moments*, Klein documents intimate mementos of a specific place and time that are easily overlooked. And by recording them visually, she gives them significance, acknowledging the aforementioned overlooked as a newfound thing of beauty.

She is also the creator of the *Broken Circle—Children of Divorce and Separation* project, which combines her photographs with narrative.

Klein's work is widely exhibited, most recently in Santo Domingo, Dominican Republic, and it is in numerous private and public collections, including recent acquisition by the University of Minnesota's Boynton Healthcare Collection, the Minneapolis Collaborative Law Institute, Four Pillars Health, Lakewood Ranch, Florida, and the Sarasota Ritz Carlton. Her images have appeared in numerous editions of *INÚTIL Revista*, a Portuguese photography and literary publication.

Her publications, available at Amazon.com, include:

In Focus, Out of Memory

Key Moments, Discoveries at Siesta Key

Broken Circle—Children of Divorce and Separation

Her photography can be seen at www.karenklein.com

and the Broken Circle project at www.brokencircleproject.org

For additional information, please email: Karen@karenklein.com

APPENDIX

Chakra Colors and Correspondences

First Chakra: The Root chakra is our past lives, ancestry, grounding, stability, security, and basic needs. It is located at the base of the spine, the pelvic floor, and the first three vertebrae. The color is <u>Red</u>.

Second Chakra: The Sacral chakra is our level of creativity, sexual expression, and self-affirmation. It is located above the pubic bone, below the navel. The color is <u>Orange</u>.

Third Chakra: The Solar Plexus chakra is our source of personal power, will, and manifestation. It is located from the navel to the breastbone. The color is <u>Yellow</u>.

Fourth Chakra: The Heart chakra serves as a bridge connecting our body, mind, emotions, and spirit. It is our source of unconditional love, rebirth, success, growth, prosperity, development, and balance. It is located in the center of our chest. The color is <u>Green</u>.

Fifth Chakra: The Throat chakra is our source of verbal expression, communication, and the ability to speak our highest truth. It is located in the center of the throat. The color is <u>Blue</u>.

Sixth Chakra: The Third Eye chakra is our center of intuition, divine energy, and knowledge of Higher Self. The color is <u>Indigo</u>.

Seventh Chakra: The Crown chakra is enlightenment: spiritual connection to our higher selves, others, and ultimately, to the divine. This chakra is often pictured as a lotus flower opening to allow spiritual awakening in an individual. It is located at the top of the head. The color is <u>Violet.</u>

Printed in the United States
By Bookmasters